Welcome to the CAFE Workshop. We've prepared this collection of forms, quotes, and questions to help you apply what you've learned when you return to the classroom. It's easy to lose handouts when they are single pages of materials, and we hope the bound format helps you keep the materials at your fingertips for instant access.

We've designed this collection to be more than just a random set of pages culled from our workshop presentation today. We know our workshops are fast-paced, and that is by design. Many participants travel a long distance at considerable expense to attend the CAFE Workshop. We think you deserve to hear as much as possible of our latest thinking, new stories from classrooms we visit, and the most current versions of planning and instruction guides at these day-long events. Although our workshops are interactive, there isn't time for all questions from all participants to be answered. We are doing most of the talking, and the limits of the format mean you spend a lot of time listening and trying to absorb new learning. If we're doing our job well, you should have scores of new questions emerging all day long about how best to implement or revise CAFE in your classroom.

The text you hold has reflection questions sprinkled throughout the pages—more than a workbook, this is a "thinkbook" designed to help you pause and reflect on the learning from today's presentations. Even if you can't talk back to us in the midst of presenting, these reflection questions should help you "talk back" to the ideas from the workshop, wrestling with how to make them your own. You'll notice as we present today that there are many examples, stories, and materials shared from teachers who have taken our ideas about CAFE and let us know what works well, what they've tweaked, and what adaptations work best in the diverse classrooms throughout the world now using CAFE.

You can use the reflection sheets included in this book as you ponder how to implement the learning from the workshop on your own. They are also helpful when you are collaborating with a colleague or grade-level team on the implementation of CAFE. The teachers who attend our workshops are phenomenally skilled, so we know the hardest work in front of you will be to adapt our ideas to suit your students. When you are already doing your job well, it's a complex task to layer new learning and routines into a classroom where learners are already thriving. We're hoping this resource helps you in that journey of integrating the learning from the CAFE Workshop into your room, and we are so honored you are finding a place for our work in your teaching. Happy reading, happy thinking, and happy learning!

Educational Design, LLC, 1911 SW Campus Drive #683, Federal Way, WA 98023
www.thedailycafe.com

Library of Congress Cataloging in Publication Data Pending

ISBN 978-1-60155-030-9

Cover and interior design by Martha Drury
Manufactured in the United States of America

Contents

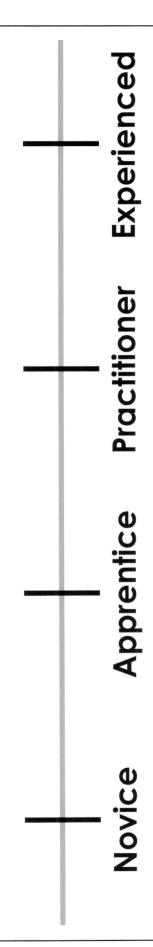

CAFE Learning Line

Novice   Apprentice   Practitioner   Experienced

Graphic 1

Where Are You on the CAFE Learning Line?

Are you more or less experienced than your colleagues?

How will/can more experienced teachers support novices?

What structures might administrators put in place to provide more support?

CAFE Menu/System/Guide for Instruction

Menu

A mechanism (visual aid) to help students learn how to elicit reading processes and strategies during each reading experience.

System

Helps teachers assess, understand, synthesize, and transfer data for instruction into their conferring notebook (The Pensieve).

Guide

Once CAFE assessments are completed, they are used to guide individual, small-group, and whole-class instruction.

The CAFE Menu

Comprehension
I understand what I read

Strategies

Use prior knowledge to connect with text

Make and adjust predictions; use text to confirm

Infer and support with evidence

Make a picture or mental image

Monitor and fix up:
Check for understanding
Back up and reread

Ask questions throughout the reading process

Use text features (titles, headings, captions, graphic features)

Summarize text; include sequence of main events

Use main idea and supporting details to determine importance

Determine and analyze author's purpose and support with text

Recognize literacy elements (genre, plot, character, setting, problem/resolution, theme)

Recognize and explain cause-and-effect relationships

Compare and contrast within and between text

Accuracy
I can read the words

Strategies

Abundant easy reading

Look carefully at letters and words

Cross checking . . .
Do the pictures and/or words look right? Do they sound right? Do they make sense?

Flip the sound

Use the pictures . . .
Do the words and pictures match?

Use beginning and ending sounds

Blend sounds; stretch and reread

Chunk letters and sounds together

Skip the word, then come back

Trade a word/guess a word that makes sense

Recognize words at sight

Fluency
I can read accurately, with expression, and understand what I read

Strategies

Voracious reading

Read appropriate-level texts that are a good fit

Reread text

Practice common sight words and high-frequency words

Adjust and apply different reading rates to match text

Use punctuation to enhance phrasing and prosody (end marks, commas, etc.)

Read text as the author would say it, conveying the meaning or feeling

Expand Vocabulary
I know, find, and use interesting words

Strategies

Voracious reading

Tune in to interesting words and use new vocabulary in speaking and writing

Use prior knowledge and context to predict and confirm meaning

Use pictures, illustrations, and diagrams

Use word parts to determine the meaning of words (prefixes, suffixes, origins, abbreviations, etc.)

Ask someone to define the word for you

Use dictionaries, thesauruses, and glossaries as tools

Behaviors That Support Reading

Get started right away	Work quietly	Select and read good-fit books
Stay in one spot	Read the whole time	Increase stamina

Sample Ready Reference Guide

Goal: **Accuracy**	Strategy: **Cross Checking . . . Do the Pictures and/or Words Look Right? Do They Sound Right? Do They Make Sense?**
Definition	Cross Checking is a strategy for ensuring the words (and sometimes pictures) make sense and match the letters on the page.
Why Children Need This Strategy	When what is read doesn't sound right or make sense. When students come to a word they don't know.
Secret to Success	Must be able to monitor for meaning and know when it is necessary to pause and fix up the meaning instead of just continuing to read. Constantly grounding reading in meaning is vital to the success of this strategy.
How We Teach It	We have found that the best way to teach this strategy is by guiding children to stop at the end of a sentence when what they read didn't make sense. We ask them to go back and find the word that was confusing. We give them highlighter tape or a special pointer to mark the word. We may also supply a sticky or even a clear acetate sheet and marking pen to lay over the text and circle the word. Once the word has been identified, we spend time teaching children the movements to go with Cross Checking: "Does the word I am reading match the letters written or the picture?" (Here they cross their right arm over their body so the right hand touches the left shoulder.) "Does it sound right?" (Left arm crosses over the body so the left hand touches their right shoulder.) Finally, "Does it make sense?" (Both arms come down with hands pointing to the ground.) By giving a kinesthetic motion to the strategy, children are more apt to remember the questions that go with it. Teaching and modeling this strategy over and over all year long so children get into the habit of using it will help them learn to become readers who self-monitor their reading by stopping when it doesn't make sense and cross checking. Language we use: "While reading, ask yourself, 'Does what I am saying match the picture and/or words? Does it sound right and does it make sense?'"
Troubleshooting	For this strategy to be viable for beginning readers, they must • read pictures, • know some letters and some sounds, • know the location of the beginning of a word. For advanced readers to be successful with Cross Checking, they must • understand decoding of word parts. If a child has difficulty with this strategy, break down the process: • stop when meaning breaks down, • look and say the letters, and the word chunks in words, • use picture support. Cross Checking is an accuracy strategy on the CAFE Menu but is also a comprehension strategy that supports children when meaning breaks down. This strategy is one of the first we teach once children have a command over the accuracy strategy Use the Picture. From the first few moments with text, students are asked to cross-check what they are reading, which requires them to constantly think and monitor meaning.

CAFE Menu for Emergent Readers

Comprehension
I listen to and understand stories that are read to me

Listen with understanding

Retell familiar stories using the pictures

Tell a connected story using pictures

Retell story, including:

- story line—characters;
- setting, problem or goal events, sequencing beginning, middle, end

Respond to questions about the story

Accuracy
I hear, work, and play with spoken language

Recognize when two words rhyme

Produce rhyming words

Orally blend words presented in syllable segments

Clap words in a sentence

Clap syllables in one to three segments

Blend onset and rime

Orally match words that begin with the same sound

Orally match words that end with the same sound

Identify the first sound in a word

Identify the last sound in a word

Blend two sounds to make a word

Blend three sounds to make a word

Segment three sounds in a word

Fluency
I know letters, sounds, and words

Recognize uppercase letters

Recognize lowercase letters

Recognize sight words

Expand Vocabulary
I am aware of print and how to handle a book

Identify front and back of book

Know where to begin reading

Know to start reading at the top of a page

Know sentences and words are read left to right

When finished with left page, move on to right page

Know return sweep when reading a sentence

Word-by-word matching

Understand concept of a word

Understand concept of a letter

Know there are spaces between words

Know the meaning of a period

Behaviors That Support Beginning Reading

Get started right away   Stay in one spot   Work quietly   Read the whole time   Increase stamina

CAFE Menu for Transitional Readers

Comprehension
I understand what I hear and read

Check for understanding
Connect to the story
Back up and reread
Predict what happens next
Identify fiction and nonfiction
Name the characters
Retell beginning, middle, end
Name the problem-solution
Name the author's purpose

Accuracy
I can read letters, sounds, and words

Cross-check ... double-check
Use the pictures
Know letters and sounds
Play with rhyming words
Identify beginning and ending sounds
Stretch or blend sounds in words
Flip the sound
Chunk letters and sounds

Fluency
I use all my skills to read

Be a voracious reader!
Know many words by heart
Read smoothly
Read with expression and pacing
Practice and read again
Read good-fit books

Expand Vocabulary
I learn new words

Be a voracious reader!
Listen for interesting words
Use interesting words
Use word tools

Behaviors That Support Reading

| Get started right away | Stay in one spot | Work quietly | Read the whole time | Increase stamina | Select and read good-fit books |

The CAFE™ Menu

Clicking on any strategy below takes you to a page
dedicated to videos, downloads, articles and books that support that strategy.
Want to see everything there is under Comprehension or Accuracy or Fluency or Expand Vocabulary?
Click on the large orange headers. The CAFE Menu

Comprehension *I understand what I read*	Accuracy *I can read the words*	Fluency *I can read accurately, with expression and understand what I read*	Expand Vocabulary *I know, find and use interesting words*
Strategies	**Strategies**	**Strategies**	**Strategies**
Check for understanding	Cross Checking... do the pictures and/or words look right? Does it sound right? Does it make sense?	Voracious reading	Voracious reading
Back up and reread		Reread text	Tune in to interesting words and use new vocabulary in my speaking and writing
Monitor and fix up	Use the picture... do the words and pictures match?	Read appropriate level texts that are a "good fit"	
Retell the story			Use pictures, illustrations, and diagrams
Use prior knowledge to connect with text	Use beginning sounds and ending sounds	Practice common sight words and high-frequency words	
Make a picture or mental image	Blend sounds, stretch and read	Adjust and apply different reading rates to match text	Use word parts to determine meaning of words (prefixes, suffixes, origins, abbreviations)
Ask questions throughout the reading process	Flip the sound	Use punctuation to enhance phrasing and prosody (end marks, commas, etc)	
Predict what will happen, use text to confirm	Chunk letters and sounds together		Use prior knowledge and context to predict and confirm meaning
Infer and support with evidence	Skip the word, then come back		
Use text features (titles, headings, captions, graphic features)	Trade a word/guess a word that makes sense		Ask someone to define the word for you
Summarize text, include sequence of main events			Use dictionaries, thesauruses and glossaries as tools
Use main idea and supporting details to determine importance			
Determine and analyze author's purpose and support with text			
Recognize literary elements (genre, plot, character, setting, problem/resolution)			
Recognize and explain cause and effect relationships			

Whole-Group Instruction Curriculum Calendar

Month:		Week 1	Week 2	Week 3	Week 4
	Phonics				
	Accuracy				
	Comprehension Skill				
	Comprehension Strategy				
	WASL Question Stem				
	Fluency				
	Writing Skill				
	Writing Workshop				
	Math				

Whole-Group Instruction Curriculum Calendar

Month:	Week 1	Week 2	Week 3	Week 4
Phonics	/a/ -afe, -ave, -aze	/ou/ -ound, -ow, -own		
Accuracy	Reread to clarify meaning of word 1.2.2	Reread to clarify meaning of word 1.2.2	Use prefixes, suffixes, and abbreviations to determine the meaning of the word. 1.2.2	Use prefixes, suffixes, and abbreviations to determine the meaning of the word. 1.2.2
Comprehension Skill	**2.2.3 Understand story elements** • Describe physical traits of characters and tell how they act. • Retell the important events of a story. • Describe the setting of a story. • Identify the speaker/narrator in a story.	**2.2.3 Understand story elements** • Describe physical traits of characters and tell how they act. • Retell the important events of a story. • Describe the setting of a story. • Identify the speaker/narrator in a story.	**2.2.3 Understand story elements** • Describe physical traits of characters and tell how they act. • Retell the important events of a story. • Describe the setting of a story. • Identify the speaker/narrator in a story.	• Organize summary information from informational/expository text and/or literary/narrative text into a teacher-provided graphic organizer to enhance text comprehension. Summarize the text. 2.1.7
Comprehension Strategy	• Identify the main idea of informational/expository passage and support with text-based evidence with teacher guidance.	• Identify the main idea of informational/expository passage and support with text-based evidence with teacher guidance.	• Identify the main idea of informational/expository passage and support with text-based evidence with teacher guidance.	Author's Viewpoint (not until 3rd grade)
MSD Question Stem	In your own words, write a summary of the story. Include three main events from the story in your selection. LC02	In your own words, write a summary of the story. Include three main events from the story in your selection. LC02	In your own words, write a summary of the story. Include three main events from the story in your selection. LC02	What is the author's purpose for writing the story? Provide three details from the story to support your answer. LT08
Fluency	Reread to make it smooth. 1.4.2	Reread to make it smooth. 1.4.2	I read, you read the same words. 1.4.2	I read, you read the same words. 1.4.2
Writing Skill	Interview Questions	Interview Questions	Interview Questions	Interview Questions
Writing Workshop	Community Presentations	Community Presentations	Community Presentations	Community Presentations
Math Lessons: 10.9–11.10	Game: Multiplication Draw		Game: Beat the Calculator	

Structure of Daily 5 and CAFE

Focus Lesson   **7–10 minutes**

Student Choices

Read to Self
Work on Writing
Read to Someone
Listen to Reading
Word Work

Teacher Choices

Individual Conferring
Guided Groups
Assessing

20–30 Minutes

1 Guided Group
3–4 Individual Conferences

Focus Lesson   **7–10 minutes**

Student Choices

Read to Self
Work on Writing
Read to Someone
Listen to Reading
Word Work

Teacher Choices

Individual Conferring
Guided Groups
Assessing

20–30 Minutes

1 Guided Group
3–4 Individual Conferences

Focus Lesson   **7–10 minutes**

Student Choices

Read to Self
Work on Writing
Read to Someone
Listen to Reading
Word Work

Teacher Choices

Individual Conferring
Guided Groups
Assessing

20–30 Minutes

1 Guided Group
3–4 Individual Conferences

Focus Lesson   **7–10 minutes**

Historical Overview of Instruction

	1970s	1980s	1990s	Now
Purpose	We will all get through the story.	Kids must feel good about themselves. We will all get through the story with help.	Every child deserves to be taught on their level at some time during the day.	Students learn reading strategies to access text.
Resource	Basal One anthology	Basal One anthology Class sets of trade books.	Basal anthology trade books children could read	Basal anthology "leveled books" book rooms library books of choice
Classroom Library	None	100 Books	Larger, leveled	Goal of over 1,000 books in each class library, organized by genre.
Grouping	Whole-group Reading groups	Whole-group heterogeneous groups	Whole-group guided reading. walk to read	Whole group small group guiding readers one on one
Access to Text	Round robin. student might not be able to read the text.	Round robin. student might not be able to read the text.	Each student reads text he or she can read.	Teach skills and strategies so student can read any text. Each student has text he or she can read independently.

Daily 5

We no longer teach just literature . . . we teach literacy!
—Kelly Gallagher, *Readicide*

What is the difference between teaching literature and teaching literacy?

How confident are you in your ability to teach literacy on a scale of 1 to 10? Explain why you chose the number you did.

What aspects of the CAFE system might help you move up on the scale?

Which assessments do you rarely refer to in your teaching?

How might the CAFE system be integrated into your current assessment scheme?

Any assessment is only as good as the action that arises from it.
—Mary James, *Using Assessment for School Improvements*

Which assessment (outside of the CAFE system) do you use now that is most closely tied to your instruction?

How is this assessment diagnostic? Please explain.

Why has this assessment been helpful?

What have you learned from this assessment that you can apply to your use of CAFE to ensure success in your classroom?

7 Steps from Assessment to Instruction

1. Assess individual student.

2. Discuss findings with student.

3. Set goal and identify strategies with student.

4. Student declares goal on menu and in notebook.

5. Teacher fills out individual conferring sheet.

6. Teacher fills out strategy group forms.

7. Ready for instruction.

The CAFE Menu 6-5-4-3

Comprehension
I understand what I read

Strategies
- Use prior knowledge to connect with text
- Make and adjust predictions; use text to confirm
- Infer and support with evidence
- Make a picture or mental image
- Monitor and fix up:
  - Check for understanding
  - Back up and reread
- Ask questions throughout the reading process
- Use text features (titles, headings, captions, graphic features)
- Summarize text; include sequence of main events
- Use main idea and supporting details to determine importance
- Determine and analyze author's purpose and support with text
- Recognize literacy elements (genre, plot, character, setting, problem/resolution, theme)
- Recognize and explain cause-and-effect relationships
- Compare and contrast within and between text

Accuracy
I can read the words

Strategies
- Abundant easy reading
- Look carefully at letters and words
- Cross checking . . . :
  - Do the pictures and/or words I am using. Do they sound right? Do they make sense?
- Use the pictures . . . :
  - Do the words and pictures match?
- Use beginning and ending sounds
- Blend sounds and reread
- Chunk letters and sounds together
- Skip the word, then come back
- Trade a word/guess a word that makes sense
- Recognize words at sight

Fluency
I can read accurately, with expression, and understand what I read

Strategies
- Voracious reading
- Read appropriate-level texts that are a good fit
- Reread text
- Practice common sight words and high-frequency words
- Adjust and apply different reading rate to match text
- Use punctuation to enhance phrasing and prosody (end marks, commas, etc.)
- Read text as the author would say it, conveying the meaning or feeling

Expand Vocabulary
I know, find, and use interesting words

Strategies
- Voracious reading
- Tune in to interesting words and use new vocabulary in speaking and writing
- Use prior knowledge and context to predict and confirm meaning
- Use pictures, illustrations, and diagrams
- Use word parts to determine the meaning of words (prefixes, suffixes, origins, abbreviations, etc.)
- Ask someone to define the word
- Use dictionaries, thesauruses, and glossaries as tools

Behaviors That Support Reading

Get started right away	Stay in one spot	Work quietly	Read the whole time	Increase stamina	Select and read good-fit books

From Assessment to Conferring: Sample Needs and Strategies

What We Are Seeing	Potential Goals	Possible Strategy	Alternative Strategy
Reading too quickly	Fluency	Adjust and apply different reading rates to match text	Phrasing, use punctuation
Leaving off ends of words	Accuracy	Cross checking	Chunk letters together
Little expression, lacks prosody, and omits punctuation	Fluency	Phrasing, using punctuation	Voracious reading
Can't remember what was read	Comprehension	Check for understanding	Retell or summarize Make a picture or mental image Determine importance using theme, main ideas, and supporting details
Stalls on words	Accuracy	Skip the word, then come back	Blend sounds; stretch and reread
Student jumps right into reading story, then lacks understanding	Comprehension	Use prior knowledge to connect with text	Ask questions while reading Make connections to text
Doesn't remember details but understands the main idea	Comprehension	Retell the story	Recognize literary elements
Doesn't stick with a book	Reading Behaviors Book Selection	Read appropriate-level text Choose good-fit books	Voracious reading
Chooses books that are too hard	Reading Behaviors Fluency Expand Vocabulary Comprehension Accuracy	Read appropriate-level text	Ask, Does this make sense?
Can comprehend literally but can't read between the lines	Comprehension	Infer and support with evidence	Ask questions while reading Predict what will happen; use text to confirm
Reads words with correct letters but wrong sounds	Accuracy	Flip the sound	Cross checking
Sounds out each individual letter	Accuracy	Chunk letters together	Blend sounds
Beginning reader, knows few words but most letter sounds	Fluency Accuracy	Practice common sight words and high-frequency words	Blend sounds; stretch and reread
Doesn't remember details from nonfiction	Comprehension	Use text features (titles, headings, captions, graphic features)	Determine and analyze author's purpose and support with text
Doesn't understand the text because does not understand key word in selection	Expand Vocabulary	Tune in to interesting words	Reread to clarify the meaning of a word Ask someone to define the word for you

Reflective Follow-Up for Grade-Level Teams and Professional Learning Groups

Try out the form From Assessment to Conferring: Sample Needs and Strategies in your classroom and bring notes and observations to a meeting with colleagues. Discuss together:

What worked well?

What different patterns did you observe with your own students?

What might you do differently the next time you use the form?

How has your discussion with colleagues changed your thinking about the form?

Reading Conferring Sheet

Name _____

Goals

•

•

Strengths

•

•

	Observation and Instruction	Next Steps to Meet Goal
Date Touch Point		
Date Touch Point		
Date Touch Point		
Date Touch Point		
Date Touch Point		
Date Touch Point		

Reading Conferring Sheet

Name _____

My Goal: My Many Strengths:

My Strategy:

My Goal: What I may work on next . . .

My Strategy:

Next Steps to Meet Goal		Next Steps to Meet Goal	
Date Touch Point		Date Touch Point	
Date Touch Point		Date Touch Point	
Date Touch Point		Date Touch Point	
Date Touch Point		Date Touch Point	
Date Touch Point		Date Touch Point	
Date Touch Point		Date Touch Point	

Reading Conferring Sheet with Icons

Name _____

Goals   Strengths

- •   - •

- •   - •

	Observation and Instruction	Next Steps to Meet Goal
Date Touch Point		
Date Touch Point		
Date Touch Point		
Date Touch Point		
Date Touch Point		
Date Touch Point		

Reading Conferring Sheet with Icons

Name *Jennie*

Goals and Strategies

- Accuracy—Chunk Sounds and Letters Together
-

Strengths

- Listening Comprehension
-

Date		Observation and Instruction		Next Steps to Meet Goal
Date 2/8 **Touch Point**	✎ 👁 ⚙	Jot down the title of the selection. Observe . . . What do I notice related to the goal? Think : . . . Do I teach or reinforce what we planned yesterday? Or change the plan based on what I see today?	🎯 **Next**	Give child 2 "targets" each day 1. Comprehension—Think about your reading and what is happening in your selection. 2. Practice strategy. AND Plan for tomorrow.
Date 2/9 **Touch Point**	✎ 👁 ⚙	Jennie read Super Fly Guy. She came to 3 words she didn't know. She just guessed the words and went on. Teach her how to chunk sounds and letters together. Stop and check for understanding.	🎯 **Next**	1. Think about what you are reading! 2. In your Reader's Notebook, log all the words you come across that you don't know and can use with this strategy. Next, we will review the words in your notebook and watch you using this strategy in your reading. Let's set an appointment to meet back tomorrow. (Write on calendar.)
Date 2/10 **Touch Point**	✎ 👁 ⚙	Super Fly Guy While reading came to 2 words, was able to chunk one word, could chunk the next word but couldn't "say it fast." Identified the word she read using the strategy. Restated how she used the strategy. Teach how to fix the last word by chunking sounds together.	🎯 **Next**	1. Think about reading. 2. Continue to write words in notebook she is chunking. Review notebook, see if she is transferring it to her reading.
Date 2/11 **Touch Point**	✎ 👁 ⚙	Space Race Read fluently, came to the word "wrong," chunked and moved on. Seems like she has ahold of the strategy but not all words work with chunking. Watch for "flip the sound." She is not using the correct vowels. (Shipes for Ships) Modeled flip the sound with ship, so when chunking, she may need to flip until it makes sense.	🎯 **Next**	1. Think about reading. Comprehend. 2. Use a sticky note while reading to record the words she is using the strategy with. See if she can flip the sound if it doesn't make sense. Check the notes and see if flipping the sound is helping with chunking.
Date **Touch Point**	✎ 👁 ⚙		🎯 **Next**	
Date **Touch Point**	✎ 👁 ⚙		🎯 **Next**	

Strategy Groups and Instruction

Goal	Strategy		Names	Touch Points	Individual Conferring Touch Points
Date	Lesson				

Goal	Strategy		Names	Touch Points	Individual Conferring Touch Points
Date	Lesson				

Goal	Strategy		Names	Touch Points	Individual Conferring Touch Points
Date	Lesson				

Observation Sheet

Purpose of Observation

Time	What I See and Hear	My Thoughts

Productive, Effective, Focused Teaching and Learning

1. Check calendar for appointments.
2. Prepare (30 seconds)
   Review your conferring notes for the student's strengths and strategy focus.
3. 👁 Observe (1 minute) *"[Student], please read so I can listen in; then tell me about yourself as a reader."*
   Observe the student. Is he or she applying the skill/strategy taught or reinforced last time you met?
   What is the student doing well with his or her strategy/skill application?
   Record this on the conferring sheet.
4. 🧠 Reinforce and Teach (1 minute)
   I noticed _____ ; what did you notice? Today we are going to _____."
   Verbally share with student your observations of what he or she was doing well.
   Teach or reinforce the skill or strategy you feel is just right for the student now by
   - explicit explanation,
   - modeling,
   - thinking aloud,
   - offering advice.
5. Practice (1 minute) *"Now it is your turn. You try . . . "*
   Ask the student to practice the skill/strategy while you listen in.
6. 🔊 Plan (30 seconds) *"This is what I am hearing, and because of that, this may be our next step."*
   Next Based on today's teaching and learning, decide and agree together what the next step will be. It isn't uncommon for students to need continued practice with the previous strategy.
   Write this plan on the coaching sheet.
7. Encourage (15 seconds)
   Just before you leave the student, encourage him or her to continue to practice the skill taught or reinforced today.
   Student should articulate the goal.

- The times above serve as guidelines, and though it isn't necessary to strictly adhere to them, they will give you a general idea so you can keep your conferences focused and brief.
- Each step above may be shorter or longer, depending on what the child is doing that day, and where you are in the gradual release of teaching the skills or strategies to the student.
- Remember that brief, focused conferences that occur frequently are considerably more beneficial than sporadic, lengthy ones.

Observation Sheet

Purpose of Observation

Different Levels, Same Skill?

Time	What I See and Hear	My Thoughts

Goal _Comprehension_	Strategy _Check for Understanding_	Names	Touch Points	Individual Conferring Touch Points
Date	**Lesson**			
11-4	Introduce Strategy and Secret	Quintion	2, 3, 3	
	Model with "Incredible Life of Riley"—3 times			
	Students practice in own books			
	Review strategy—Kirsten modeled	Lena		
	Assign—practice strategy in own book			
	Meet tomorrow			
11-5	Observe—review strategy			
	Each student read 1 sentence and model strategy	Micha	1, 22	
	Review—assign sticky notes			
	Meet tomorrow			
11-6	Review and model each practice—meet 2 days	Kirsten	1–2, 2, 2	1, 2, 3, 2

Goal	Strategy	Names	Touch Points	Individual Conferring Touch Points
Date	**Lesson**			

Goal	Strategy	Names	Touch Points	Individual Conferring Touch Points
Date	**Lesson**			

Reading Conferring Sheet

Name *Kirsten*

Goals *Comprehension*
- *Check for Understanding*
-

Strengths
- *Fluency*
-

	Observation and Instruction	Next Steps to Meet Goal
Date 11-4 Touch Point 1	"Danny Goes to the Park" continues to read—doesn't stop Practice and model secret practices 2 times together	Partner-read with Micah Stop and check together Meet tomorrow
Date 11-5 Touch Point 2	"Danny's Red Shoes" Was aware to stop—and do secret. Think aloud . . . Here is what you did . . . Continue to practice	Partner-read seems to be helping Meet with Micah Meet in 2 days
Date 11-7 Touch Point 3	"Danny's Cape" Stopped at end of each page. Could say who and what. Identified what she did.	Partner read Meet in 2 days
Date 11-11 Touch Point 2	"Geologist Danny" Read quickly—no stopping Offered advice—stop Could ✔ for understanding with prompting	Add stickies to each page—reminder to stop Meet tomorrow
Date 11-12 Touch Point 3	"Get Down Danny" Stopped often—remembers who and what Stickies helped her remember	Continue stickies Meet in 2 days
Date 11-14 Touch Point 3	"Danny's Red Socks" Stops often— Add a harder book—	Take away stickies Meet in 2 days

Conferring Sheet with Icons

Name __Jennie__

Goals and Strategies
- Accuracy—Chunk Sounds and Letters Together
- Next strategy—Flip the Sound?

Strengths
- Listening Comprehension
-

	Observation and Instruction	Next Steps to Meet Goal
Date 2/13 **Touch Point** 1	Mr. Whisper Chunked 2 words Worked on blends—bl, gr	1. Comprehension—think 2. Practice blending sounds—bl, gr **Next** Check beginning blends
Date 2/15 **Touch Point** 1	The Wind Blows Strong Has beginning blends (onset) Missing ending blends (rime) Focus on ending blend spl osh	1. Check for Understanding 2. Stickie words with ending chunk **Next** Check rimes
Date 2/17 **Touch Point** 2	The Secret of Spooky House Read spooky—wow Stickied 3 words Starting to see chunks Reviewed and practiced chunks	1. Think 2. Continue to stickie **Next** Watch for vowel sounds
Date 2/18 **Touch Point** 3	The Secret of Spooky House Stickied 3 words Start to fade out instruction	1. Retell 2. Think about chunks and when it works **Next** Appointment in 3 days Think about flip sounds
Date **Touch Point**		**Next**
Date **Touch Point**		**Next**

Touch Points monitor teaching and document student learning.

1. Below Standard

2. Approaching Standard

3. Meeting Standard

4. Exceeding Standard

3
Teaching Attempts

1 or 2
Touch Points

Materials

Teaching
Explicit Explanation
Model
Think Aloud
Offer Advice

Change Something

Setting

4 or 5
Observations

3 or 4
Touch Points

Understanding Touch Points

Touch Points:
Determining When a Child Is Ready
for a New CAFE Menu Strategy

How do we determine if a child is ready to move to a new strategy on the CAFE menu? Touch Points!

We call it a "touch point" when we see a student correctly execute a strategy while reading. We either make note of the date the child successfully used the strategy or put a check mark in the margin of the conferring sheet. Once these total four or five, we determine whether or not the child has competently added it to the repertoire of strategies they have control of. If so, we place a check mark and date next to this strategy on their CAFE menu, indicating they have command of the strategy. We also place a check mark and date in the date/touch point box on the conferring form and/or the strategy group page, signaling the end to the teaching and coaching support for this particular strategy. Before the conference ends, we look at the CAFE menu and determine which strategy to highlight and focus on next.

An alternative to check marks would be actual grades. For example, if a child's goal is comprehension and their strategy is check for understanding, the first day we meet with them to introduce this strategy we would write a "1" in the touch point box on their conferring sheet since they are below standard with this skill. The next time we meet we might notice they are starting to understand and use the skill, so we give them a "2," meaning they are approaching standard. We assess their knowledge and application of the skill each time we meet together, putting the correct number (or letter grade) in each time. For our district, a "3" means the child is meeting standard and a "4" is exceeding standard. As we look over our record sheets, we know we can move a child on to another strategy when they have accumulated four or five 3s and 4s.

It doesn't matter whether you use check marks, alphabetical grades, or a numerical system: when a child has successfully demonstrated the skill four or five times and you feel they have really internalized it, you can phase out direct instruction, continue to monitor periodically, and move to a new skill or strategy.

Calendar

SUN	MON	TUE	WED	THU	FRI	SAT

October

*Group

SUN	MON	TUE	WED	THU	FRI	SAT
					1 Assess	2
3	4	5 Assess	6 Assess	7 Assess	8 Assess	9
10	11 Darrah Will	12 Darrah Jade *Fluency	13 Darrah Will Jade *Accuracy *Vocab	14 Darrah *Accuracy *Fluency	15 Darrah Will *Accuracy *Comprehension	16
17	18 Jade *Accuracy *Fluency	19 Will *Accuracy	20 *Accuracy *Vocab	21 Will *Accuracy *Fluency	22 Will Sebastian Jade *Comprehension	23
24	25 *Accuracy *Vocab	26 Will Sebastian *Accuracy	27 Jade *Accuracy *Fluency	28 Will Sebastian Jade *Accuracy	29 Sebastian *Comprehension	30

Keeping Track

Reading Level Data

	Independent	Instructional	Frustration	Independent	Instructional	Frustration	Growth	Independent	Instructional	Frustration	Independent	Instructional	Frustration	Growth

Writing Conferring Sheet

Name _____

Goals   Strengths

-
-

	Observation and Instruction	Next Steps to Meet Goal
Date Touch Point		
Date Touch Point		
Date Touch Point		
Date Touch Point		
Date Touch Point		
Date Touch Point		

Please indicate areas where you would like support.

❑ **Daily 5:** Set up Read to Self, including support lessons
❑ **Daily 5:** Set up Work on Writing, including support lessons
❑ **Daily 5:** Set up Read to Someone, including support lessons
❑ **Daily 5:** Set up Word Work, including support lessons
❑ **Daily 5:** Set up Listen to Reading, including support lessons
❑ **Daily 5:** Barometer Child
❑ **Daily 5:** Planning Foundation Lessons

❑ **Student Choice:** Building Stamina
❑ **Student Choice:** Handing off Daily 5 choice to students
❑ **Student Choice:** Supporting student book choice
❑ **Student Choice:** Supporting student writing choice

❑ **Assessing:** Administering reading assessments
❑ **Assessing:** Analyzing assessment data and setting student goals
❑ **Assessing:** Setting up assessment materials and student assessment box

❑ **Whole Group:** Develop Curriculum Calendar
❑ **Whole Group:** Using CAFE and Curriculum Calendar to design lessons
❑ **Whole Group:** Understanding interactive read-aloud, teaching skills and strategies

CAFE Strategy: Cross Checking

When reading a book for pleasure or for information, chances are you will come to a word or two you are unsure of. You probably will use the accuracy strategy of **cross checking** without even thinking about it because it is second nature to you as a reader to read accurately. Accuracy is not second nature to children learning to read. It is something that needs to be taught using a variety of strategies.

Your child has been introduced to the accuracy strategy of **cross checking**. It is important to slow readers down when they come to a word they don't know and teach them to apply the strategy of **cross checking** so they are able to fix the meaning and not just skip the word. **Cross checking** requires a person to constantly think and monitor meaning. It is a strategy for ensuring that the words and pictures read make sense and match the letters on a page.

How can you help your child with this strategy at home?

1. Listen to your child read. When he comes to a word he is unsure of, remind him to cross check. Ask:
   - Does the word you are reading match the picture or letters written? (*Child crosses his right arm over his body)
   - Does it sound right? (*Child crosses his left arm over his body, making an X)
   - Does it make sense? (*Both arms come down with hands pointing to the ground.)
   Doing physical movements with each question helps children to remember the questions.

2. If your child is having difficulty with this strategy at home, break down the process:
   - Have her stop reading when meaning breaks down.
   - Tell her to look at the letters and say the sounds or look for word chunks in words.
   - Remind her to use the pictures to help.

3. To make your child aware of using this strategy, give him a piece of paper and tell him to make a tally mark each time he uses the cross checking strategy.

Thank you for your continued support at home!

CAFE Strategy: Check for Understanding

Even as an adult reader, there are times when I am reading a story, get lost, and am not sure what has happened. Fortunately, when this happens, I have strategies to help me understand the story. The same thing happens when children read. However, children often keep reading and do not realize they have lost comprehension until the end of the story. They are too concerned with reading accurately, and forget to take the time to think about what they are reading. How can we help them gain comprehension? We can teach them the comprehension strategy **check for understanding,** because good readers stop frequently to check for understanding or to ask who and what.

How can you help your child with this strategy at home?

1. When reading to your child, stop periodically and say, "Let's see if we remember what I just read. Think about *who* the story was about and *what* happened." Do this 3 or 4 times throughout the story.

2. When reading to your child, stop and have them practice checking for understanding by saying, "I heard you say . . ."

3. Ask your child the following questions:
   - Who did you just read about?
   - What just happened?
   - Was your brain talking to you while you read?
   - Do you understand what was read?
   - What do you do if you don't remember?

Thank you for your continued support at home!

CAFE Strategy: Tune In to Interesting Words

When children learn to **tune in to interesting words**, they build word awareness and the understanding of words. This leaves them with "thinking power" in their brain to comprehend and make meaning of what is read. Have you ever heard a new word, looked it up, and then repeated it often to remember it? Students who **tune in to interesting words** expand their vocabulary by focusing on these new words and their meaning. By looking for words that are interesting and unique, children not only increase their vocabulary, but also enhance their comprehension. A child must be exposed to a word multiple times for it to become part of his or her vocabulary.

How can you help your child with this strategy at home?

1. Ask your child to tell you about his or her word collector at school. The word collector is a form that allows your child to keep track of interesting words found in books he or she is reading. Create a word collector at home to hang on the refrigerator or to keep in a special place.

2. When your child is reading or you are reading to your child, ask your child to find three interesting words. Have your child write these words down and talk about their meaning. See if anyone in your family is able to use the words in a sentence. Add these words to your family word collector.

3. Encourage your child to find interesting words when watching TV or in daily conversation. When your child tunes in to an interesting word, help him or her understand the word and then add it to the family word collector.

4. As always, modeling is a wonderful way to spark interest in children. When you are reading a magazine, newspaper, or book, tune in to an interesting word and discuss it with your child. Explain that even adult readers **tune in to interesting words** to better understand text.

Thank you for your continued support at home!

Comprehension

"I understand what I read"

Accuracy

"I can read the words"

Fluency

"I can read accurately, with expression, and understand what I read"

Expand Vocabulary

"I know, find, and use interesting words"

Goal: **Comprehension**	Strategy: **Check for Understanding**
Definition	A comprehension strategy that teaches children to stop frequently and check, or monitor, whether they understand what they are reading. This typically is a quick summary of what they've read, starting with "who" and "what."
Why Children Need This Strategy	Often as beginning readers, children are so aware of reading accurately that they forget to take time and think about what they are reading, checking to see whether they understand the text. Advanced readers can develop the habit of reading through text without monitoring even if they were aware of the Check for Understanding strategy as beginning readers.
Secret to Success	Knowing when we read that we must think about the story and realize what the author is trying to tell us or what we are learning from the book. Readers stop frequently to check for understanding or to ask who and what.
How We Teach It	This vital strategy is not only one of the first we introduce, but also one we model each and every day of the school year. • Modeling during our read-aloud we stop periodically and say, "Let me see if I remember what I just read. I am going to start by thinking of who the story was about and what happened." • We continue to stop periodically and talk through the "who" and "what," usually about three or four times during each read-aloud. • After two or three times of modeling this for students, we start asking them to answer the "who" and the "what" through "listen and talk," asking one student to do it for the whole class and then expecting children to do it on their own. Language we use: "Stop often to check for understanding before you read any further." "**Who** did you just read about and **what** just happened?" "How often did you stop to check for understanding? After each sentence, after each paragraph, at the end of each page?" "Was your brain talking to you while you read?" "Are you finding you are understanding what you are reading?" "What do you do if you don't remember?"
Troubleshooting	We had a parent cut out large check marks, approximately 7 inches long, from balsa wood. Often we provide these check marks to students as a reminder to stop and check for understanding. They work particularly well when partners are reading together and working on Check for Understanding. The person listening to his or her partner read has the job of holding the check mark. When the reader comes to the end of a page or paragraph, the check-mark holder checks for understanding what the reader just read. On one side of the check marks we write, "Check for Understanding" and on the other side, "Who and what."

Goal: **Accuracy**	Strategy: **Chunk Letters and Sounds Together**
Definition	Chunking letters and sounds together within a word to make decoding more efficient, rapid, and accurate.
Why Children Need This Strategy	For children to be able to understand what they read, they must be able to read the words rapidly as well as accurately. This frees children to focus their attention on the meaning of what they have read.
Secret to Success	Watch for familiar word patterns such as blends, digraphs, prefixes, suffixes, compound words, and small words within a word.
How We Teach It	This strategy is typically for students reading beyond the basic CVC level. Once they know the different sounds made by digraphs, blends, etc., we use different tools to help kids identify them in their reading. When working with a large chart or Big Book, we will use "frames" that outline the smaller word parts. These frames are everything from cardboard cut into a handheld magnifying-glass shape (sometimes complete with colored acetate glued in place of where the lens would be) to a large fly swatter with part of the middle cut out to form a frame that can be laid over a word, isolating the smaller chunk. When we are using a book as we confer with students, we teach them to use their fingers to mask off the chunks found in words, decoding those chunks first, then moving on to tackle the whole word. Slowing the process of looking for smaller parts in words helps train students' eyes to look rapidly for those chunks.
Troubleshooting	The prerequisite to this strategy is knowing and having experience with the variety of digraphs, blends, prefixes, and suffixes found in words. Beginning with our youngest students, we spend time partaking in word studies that focus on these parts of words so as to build their background knowledge and experiences. Then as the words they encounter in text become more sophisticated, they have applicable knowledge and are ready to apply this strategy.

Goal: **Accuracy**	Strategy: **Flip the Sound**
Definition	Teach children to use their knowledge of letter sounds to decode words by trying out, or "flipping," the different sounds a letter can make until they hear a word they recognize and that makes sense.
Why Children Need This Strategy	Many words in the English language don't follow conventional phonics rules. Drawing upon knowledge of the variety of sounds a letter makes can sometimes help children decode a word that has a letter that varies from the traditional sound associated with it.
Secret to Success	Being aware when a word doesn't sound right or make sense. Knowing the multiple sounds a letter or letter combination can make. Being able to flip the sounds around and then rely on comprehension to see whether the new word sounds right and makes sense. This strategy works particularly well with vowel sounds.
How We Teach It	Our favorite way to teach this strategy is by using a kinesthetic motion to remind students to flip the sound when they come to a word they don't know. Whether teaching the whole class, a small group, or an individual, we follow the same pattern: We model the strategy by showing them a word that we read incorrectly. If we are working with an individual, we wait until they read a word incorrectly and get to the end of the sentence. Then we stop them to model the strategy of Flip the Sound on their missed word. When we model the strategy, we put our hand palm-down and flip it over and say, "I think I'll try flipping the sound." We find it very important to articulate for the students that while we are flipping the sounds in a word, we must listen to see whether we recognize the word. Common language we use in lessons with Flip the Sound: "Did the word you just read sound right?" "When you flip the sound, listen for a word that you recognize." "What other sound could that letter make?"
Troubleshooting	If a student is struggling with this strategy, having a partner give them a prompt that is the kinesthetic motion of flipping over their hand can be a quiet reminder to try the strategy.

Selected Readings for Study Groups

Conferring with Children: Principles and Procedures

Just for fun, when we're in a new classroom of young children together, we often introduce ourselves and begin by asking the class a question. "Who do you think is older?" Invariably, the children choose Gail. Why? Because she is a few inches taller than Joan.

For the record, Gail is a little older than Joan (Joan is forever 29 years old, and Gail is 29 and a half). The question and response always makes us smile because it reminds us that our assumptions when we are young often prove to be wrong as we age. For children, the height of a peer is a good gauge of how old they are. For adults, not so much.

As we've worked with children over the years, we've had to change some of the assumptions we had about the best way to confer with students. Many of the assumptions we had when we were younger worked well, but it was a different environment for teaching, with different standards and accountability.

One of the hardest things for us about conferring in the beginning was truly getting up, moving about, and starting to confer with children one on one. We were accustomed to guided reading groups—staying in one area and having the children come to us for instruction. When we'd have time to confer individually, we'd call out for students to come to us or post a schedule of conferences on the board.

Getting up and moving to confer with students can be a little scary at first, but once you begin, it's exciting. The concerns we had—and many teachers share—are about time and purpose:

- How long will each of these conferences take?
- How can we stay focused, given that there is so much we might tackle with each child?
- What exactly is my role in the conference?

Rethinking Conference Protocols

The reason we confer with any student is to help them work toward individual goals. The goals come from the assessments at the start of the year or previous conferences, and they become the focus of each conference with the child.

One of the things we had to resist was creating a preset conferring form. That's what we'd become accustomed to as teachers—meeting with a child, then filling in blanks on an assessment or conferring form as we listened to them read.

The conferring forms that are provided in many assessment systems or professional books are often loaded with questions: What are you reading now? What are your strengths as a reader? Let's discuss vocabulary. What about fluency? Tell me why you chose this book, and on and on. It isn't that these aren't good questions, but there are too many of them. By the time you've conferred with two or three children, the reading workshop for the day may be over.

Although keeping good records is important to us, we've found that the best use of our time in the conference is to observe and listen closely to the child, teach and/or reinforce the strategy they are working on, have the child practice the strategy, plan for the student's next step, and encourage them to keep going. Our record-keeping forms are short, concise, and include only the information we need to refer to quickly to keep the child moving forward in reading. This way, instead of long conferences with detailed notes that may have little effect on the child's strategy work and immediate goal as a reader, we have continual brief, targeted contact and instruction with all of our students more frequently.

We are also teaching children to look more closely at where they are now as readers, and where they might go tomorrow or over the next week, in working on skills and strategies to become better readers. Many of the conference protocols we've seen and used in the past look at what children are reading at the moment, or ask them to talk about their whole life as a reader. There doesn't seem to be much in between those two extremes, but the "in between" is where we all live as teachers, trying to get students and ourselves to look at practical steps we can take today, tomorrow, and this week to move forward as readers. With conferring now, we're looking at days and weeks, rather than moments and years, to help children become more independent in tracking their progress and taking responsibility for it.

One of the benefits of setting goals with children that they work on over a period of time is that it saves time in conferences. Instead of taking time during each conference with a child to come up with a new goal or goals, the child begins with knowing he or she is working on developing fluency, or on expanding vocabulary. Starting with a pre-established focus, instead of always having to establish a focus at the beginning of the conference, saves us an enormous amount of time. We can spend far more of the limited time we have with each child observing and listening to them read, and then teaching, rather than wasting much of the first part of the conference trying to figure out what we need to concentrate on that day.

We have a focus for our next conference before we even meet with the child again. When children see us walking up to them for a conference, they mentally begin to sort through what progress they have made toward their goal, and what topics around the goal we might discuss when we meet.

Selected Readings for Study Groups

Flexible Groups: Moving Beyond Levels to Assess Reading Needs

In the past, flexible groups really weren't that flexible in our classroom, especially when we based the groups on students' reading levels. For years we said, "Yes, of course we do flexible groups!" But the truth was we didn't really know what that meant, and we certainly had no idea of how to manage those groups.

Once we started slotting kids into groups based on needing to know something more about specific reading strategies or skills like inferring or fluency, it moved us beyond levels. Many of these group meetings involve using different books, at different levels. It is the skill that focuses the group, not the level. As we assess kids in one-on-one conferences, we're looking for patterns. This is different from merely looking for levels and grouping accordingly. We look at kids who have similar needs based on comprehension, accuracy, fluency, or vocabulary, using the CAFE menu as a guide. As clusters of students with similar needs emerge, we form reading groups.

Because we regroup based on needs on a weekly basis, the groups are always shifting. There are five- through eight-year-olds in Joan's multiage K–2 classroom, so there are often a wide range of ages in each group, with reading abilities from early emergent to fluent. Children learn to expect that groups will not meet on a set schedule–some groups meet repeatedly to tackle a new skill together, other groups are one-time events to home in quickly on a specific need to interest for the students.

Even with the youngest readers, the skills needed often go beyond decoding. They are learning how to sit with others, carry on conversations about reading, and wait their turn to respond or receive support from their teachers. (When we look over our group notes, it's interesting to us that many of our groups that DO have students all at a similar level are often groups of older, more sophisticated readers.) These are the students who have mastered the basics of decoding text, and benefit from peer support to understand more complex notions of plot, character development, visual nonfiction cues, or inference.

Bibliography

Allington, Richard. 2005. *What Really Matters for Struggling Readers: Designing Research-Based Programs*. Boston, MA: Allyn and Bacon.

———. 2008. *What Really Matters in Response to Intervention: Research Based Design*. Boston, MA: Allyn and Bacon.

Allington, Richard, and Patricia Cunningham. 2010. *Classrooms That Work: They Can All Read and Write*. Boston, MA: Allyn and Bacon.

Atwell, Nancie. 1987. *In the Middle: New Understandings About Writing, Reading and Learning*. Portsmouth, NH: Heinemann.

———. 2007. *The Reading Zone: How to Help Kids Become Skilled, Passionate, Habitual, Critical Readers*. New York, NY: Scholastic.

Buckner, Aimee. 2005. *Notebook Know-How: Strategies for the Writer's Notebook*. Portland, ME: Stenhouse.

———. 2009. *Notebook Connections: Strategies for the Reader's Notebook*. Portland, ME: Stenhouse.

Duffy, Gerald. 2009. *Explaining Reading: A Resource for Teaching Concepts, Skills and Strategies*. New York, NY: Guilford Press.

Gallagher, Kelly. 2009. *Readicide: How Schools Are Killing Reading and What You Can Do About It*. Portland, ME: Stenhouse.

Gambrell, Linda, Lesley Morrow, Michael Pressley, and John Guthrie. 2007. *Best Practices in Literacy Instruction*. New York, NY: The Guilford Press.

Gladwell, Malcolm. 2008. *Outliers: The Story of Success*. Boston, MA: Little, Brown and Company.

Grinder, Michael. 1996. *Envoy: Your Personal Guide to Classroom Management*. Battle Ground, WA: Michael Grinder and Associates.

Howard, Mary. 2009. *RTI from All Sides: What Every Teacher Needs to Know*. Portsmouth, NH: Heinemann.

Johnston, Peter. 2004. *Choice Words*. Portland, ME: Stenhouse.

Miller, Donalyn. 2009. *The Book Whisperer: Awakening the Inner Reader in Every Child*. San Francisco, CA: Jossey-Bass.

Routman, Regie. 2002. *Reading Essentials: The Specifics You Need to Teach Reading Well*. Portsmouth, NH: Heinemann.

Sibberson, Franki. 2008. *Beyond Leveled Books*. Portland, ME: Stenhouse.

Sibberson, Franki, and Karen Szymusiak. 2003. *Still Learning to Read: Teaching Students in Grades 3–6*. Portland, ME: Stenhouse.

The most basic and powerful way to connect to another person is to listen. Just listen. Perhaps the most important thing we ever give each other is our attention. A loving silence often has far more power to heal and to connect than the most well-intentioned words.

—Rachel Naomi Remen

After you've done a thing the same way for two years, look it over carefully. After five years, look at it with suspicion. And after ten years, throw it away and start all over.
—Alfred Edward Pearlman

If you want to truly
understand something, try
to change it.

—Kurt Lewin

Success and failure are both greatly overrated. But failure gives you a whole lot more to talk about.
—Hildegard Knef

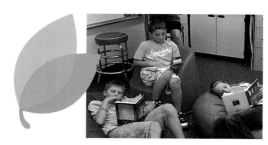

Spoon feeding, in the long
run teaches us nothing but
the shape of the spoon.
　　　　　　—E.M. Forster

Teaching reading IS rocket science.

—Louisa Moats

As the child approaches a new text he is entitled to an introduction so that when he reads, the gist of the story can provide some guide for a fluent reading.

—Marie Clay

The pleasure of all reading
is doubled when one lives
with another who shares
the same books.
 —Katherine Mansfield

The libraries have become
my candy store.
—Juliana Kimball

A desk is a dangerous place from which to view the world.

—John Le Carre

Obstacles are those
frightful things you see
when you take your eyes
off the goal.

—Henry Ford

Acceptance of prevailing
standards often means we
have no standards of our
own.

—Jean Toomer

If you are a struggling
reader, all you have to do
is look tough and say
nothing, and then you will
become invisible.
—Richard Vacca

Nobody can go back and
start a new beginning, but
anyone can start today
and make a new ending.
　　　　—Maria Robinson

True genius resides in the capacity for evaluation of uncertain, hazardous, and conflicting information.
—Winston Churchill

The doors we open and
close each day decide
the lives we live.
—Flora Whittemore

The teachers I work with
continue to assess our
thinking on assessment.
One question that guides
our conversation is "Who
will learn something if we
do this?"
—Joanne Hindley Salch

It takes a lot of courage to release the familiar and seemingly secure, to embrace the new. But there is no real security in what is no longer meaningful. There is more security in the adventurous and exciting, for in movement there is life, and in change there is power.

—Alan Cohen

Even when freshly washed
and relieved of all obvious
confections, children tend
to be sticky.
—Fran Lebowitz

What is our praise or pride
but to imagine excellence
and try to make it.
—Richard Wilbur

"It's our choices, Harry,
that show what we truly
are, far more than our
abilities."
　　　　　　　—J.K. Rowling

A book is like a garden
carried in the pocket.
　　　　　—Chinese Proverb

When we reflect on why things work for a few students, we can begin to formulate a stance toward all students, a stance based on our commitment to respect the depth of their potential and the dignity of their person.

—Robert Fried